THE TALE OF THE GODDESS

THE TAO OF THE *GODDESS*

A Feminine Voyage of Spirituality and Selfhood

JOAN R. TARPLEY

B

BERKLEY BOOKS, NEW YORK

THE TAO OF THE GODDESS: A FEMININE VOYAGE OF SPIRITUALITY AND SELFHOOD

A Berkley Book / published by arrangement with the author

PRINTING HISTORY
Berkley trade paperback edition / May 1999

The Penguin Putnam Inc. World Wide Web site address is http://www.penguinputnam.com

ISBN: 0-425-16860-3

BERKLEY®
Berkley Books are published by The Berkley Publishing Group, a division of Penguin Putnam Inc., 375 Hudson Street, New York, New York 10014. BERKLEY and the "B" design are trademarks belonging to Penguin Putnam Inc.

PRINTED IN THE UNITED STATES OF AMERICA

10 9 8 7 6 5 4 3 2 1

Foreword

This book comes to us through divine grace in action as a communication by means of channelling.

Specifically, in "New Age" thought, channelling is a word used to mean communication by an unseen (usually unseen) spiritual being whose message is transmitted to the world at large through a human being on the planet.

To be a channel, one listens and transmits verbatim, without editing, the message of the unseen spiritual being.

I feel honored and truly privileged to be a channel of the Feminine Godhead.

THE TAO
OF THE
*G*ODDESS

~ *Be anxious for nothing.* ~

For more than a year I had been immersing my soul in Goddess energy. The energy feels good, good like in warm, comforting, powerful and empowering. Very quiet, very protective.

I reached a stage where I could quieten myself and become serene by sitting and meditating on the sentence, "I am one with the Goddess energy."

Eventually, holding the sentence in my consciousness for longer periods of time led me into deep, extended meditative silence.

A morning came when I had finished my usual meditation and was simply sitting with no one single thought in my mind. A "She" said, "I have some work for you to do."

My first response was, "Who are you?" After all, even if you know on the inside that you are being addressed by a higher power, my thinking is that you are entitled to know who the higher power professes to be.

The "she" answered quietly in my heart, "Goddess."

Not yet satisfied, I asked, "Which one?" (In the metaphysical world, there are more than one goddess. So, the voice could have come from any one of many.)

She said, "The Feminine Godhead, The Goddess from whom all others take their face and shape."

"Oh," said I.

Truthfully, I was struck silent. Silent, but not for a millisecond fearful. But, what does one say when the voice speaking to you is The Feminine Godhead, The Goddess herself? If you are the tiniest bit similar to me, for a moment suspended in time, you say nothing.

When She speaks to you, you'll know her. There was a knowing inside me that the energy I had been tracking mentally for years, and soulfully merging with for over a year, had actually spoken to me in a way that I could understand. And I was not in meditation. Now what? If, and more likely when, She speaks to you, not only will you know her, you will listen.

As spiritual people, we casually speak of talking with God. We think of our conversations with God as ordinary occurrences. Speaking with The Feminine Godhead, Goddess, is now for me equally as ordinary. But that first morning of conversation did not seem ordinary at all. I sat and said absolutely nothing although I was well aware that She had spoken of work for me to do. I said nothing. She said nothing. This woman does not chatter. The silence seemed interminable. Finally, I managed, "What work do you have for me?"

"Writing a book," She said.

I was silent. She was silent. I am a devotee of the Female Deity. She has trained me in the way of silence that I never managed with the masculine God energy alone. But, She had hooked me and She knew it. I thoroughly enjoy writing and She knows me well. Finally, I asked another question, "What type of book?"

"A book of guidance on My Way," was Her response.

At that, I mentally yelped, "What? I don't know enough about Your Way to write a page, not speak of a book!"

Goddess laughed. (Her being overflows with joy.) When She laughed I felt better, but still totally inadequate. Then She said to me, "All you have to do is write it down. I will give you the guidances day by day."

Reader, I ask you, really, what does one respond to a request for use of your energy by The Godhead of your feminine self? I don't know what you would have responded or will respond.

All I could say was a meager, "OK."

My work in earnest with the Feminine Godhead energy began years ago when I meditated on and finally wrote and signed my personal Covenant With God, Goddess, All There Is: The One. As I meditated on the question of what should my covenant say, it became clear to me that I was looking at two distinct paths. Both paths came out of The One. They were parallel to each other, could merge with the other, and were dependent on the other for the full expression of each. Nevertheless, they were separate and distinct paths. One path would primarily use and express my masculine energy—the energy we commonly refer to as God. The other would primarily use and express my feminine energy—the energy we now refer to as Goddess.

Not fully realizing—who am I kidding? Not at all realizing the ramifications of what I was choosing, I chose the path that has now ultimately revealed itself as the Goddess path. It is the path of receiving, the path of magnetism with an incredibly awesome power. The other would have put me on the path of achievement, the electric path.

In hindsight, the choice of the magnetic for me was at that time close to miraculous and a choice that would ultimately change my career path.

I was at that time a successful licensed attorney engaged in the confrontational warlike battles of the courtroom. That I did not opt onto the electric path is amazing in light of my years of training and legal work.

I am still a successful licensed attorney but no longer engaged in courtroom battles. I use my legal training in a very different way: non-confrontational and enabling. I teach and write.

Changing career paths and traveling on the path of Goddess finally required me to physically uproot my home and move hundreds of miles away from the place where I was born, had married, reared my child, and lived for forty plus years. After making my decision, and after many and varied drafts, I wrote my "Convenant With The One" in its then final form.

Some of you may ask, "What is a covenant? What does it say?" A covenant is an exchange of promises. I promised to dedicate my actions, my words, and my silences to energies I designated in exchange for designated energies from The One. Before you say that there is no bargain to be made with The One, think on the concepts of self-responsibility and self-accountability.

Once you accept and begin to live the principle that you alone are responsible for your life situations and that, with a Higher Power, you are co-creator of your manifestations, you can accept the concept that you can request The One to bestow onto you specific manifestations in exchange for specific energies.

Once I had completed and signed my covenant, I sat in meditation to request The One's acceptance of my proposed energy exchange. In meditation, I received a visual symbol that my covenant was accepted and installed in my Being, Soul and Spirit.

Having lived a lot of life since I signed the covenant, I now believe a "fair" exchange of energy will always work in the universe. The benefit of a covenant is the focus it brings to your personal consciousness.

After my covenant signing, I increasingly verbalized the thought that there must undoubtedly be a feminine Godhead, a Mrs. God, if you will. Surely, I thought, if we are created in the likeness of The One, then there must be a female One just as there is a male One and they are probably a union. The more I thought it and verbalized the thought, the more I desired less war and more contemplative silence. The desire led to my career change and ultimately to this book. To be absolutely clear for you, the reader, feminine and masculine are not used in this book interchangeably to mean *woman* and *man*. Each of us on the planet has both a feminine and masculine embodiment of energy. This book teaches each of us, woman and man, how to further develop our feminine qualities.

On the first morning of my conversation with The Goddess, I knew without being told that we would begin the morning following the request of energy for the book and the guidances would require many days. There would not be a guidance each and every day. I would know when the silence meant the end of what She intended the book to say rather than it being a respite between guidances.

For close to six months, I sat quietly after my morning meditation and listened for the voice in my heart. Following the day's guidance, I went to my computer and wrote exactly what She said. Some mornings I did not understand the meaning of what She said. However, as the day would go by, I'd see the guidance in action and came to understanding. Some mornings, all I received was, "Assimilate what you have received." Some mornings I had respite days.

After the first few days, it became clear to me that Goddess opened a major principle and then followed the principle with a "how to." In the first major principle— "Accepting the Bounty of Your Soul," there was also guidance on "how it feels when you have it." This book is set up in such a manner. Each guiding principle is followed by "how to" (and in the Bounty principle "how it feels") before the next principle is opened.

I feel that an additional word here is necessary on The Feminine Godhead. She is an integral energy within the creative force. I devoutly believe in the mental-spiritual concept of God, Goddess, All That Is. God the Father, God the Son, God the Holy Spirit is only one-half of the creative energy. There is equally as real, Goddess the Mother, Goddess the Daughter and Goddess the Holy Spirit. The Holy Spirit must have both to be the Holy Spirit.

The Feminine Godhead is equally as powerful as The Masculine Godhead, equally as loving and equally as demonstrative. There is, however, a difference in the way of manifesting through the Goddess energy instead of the masculine. The Goddess way of manifesting is what this book is about. It is worth repeating that the feminine and masculine are not used in this book interchangeably to mean *woman* and *man*. Each of us on the planet has both a feminine and masculine embodiment of masculine and feminine energy. This book is about each of us, woman and man, developing our magnetic qualities.

If you begin travelling the path of Goddess, or even visiting occasionally, after you feel comfortable with unadulterated Goddess energy, meditate on the triad—woman, wife, and whore. Your clarity of understanding insight into the physical materialization of the female will intensify manyfold.

My soul rests easily in The Goddess. For all of us who desire to know her way, here follow her guidances.

ACCEPT THE BOUNTY OF YOUR SOUL.

~ *My Own Understanding* ~

There are days when I would rather not have intuition. Those are the days when I know that I know what I know, but I would rather not know because it is too soon for me to confront, without intense pain, another person's reality.

I thought it was a mistake. Surely She didn't mean *bounty*. Bounty in my mind meant a reward paid for fugitives from justice. I tried *harvest*. But my inner voice said: "But she said bounty." So I looked it up. Bounty is a derivative of a Latin root meaning "good." Bounty defined is: "Liberality in bestowing gifts and favors; generosity; bountifulness; a lack of restraint in giving."

I felt wonderful. Her first guiding principle was to accept the generous gifts of my soul.

~ *How to accept the bounty of your soul:*

1) Relax.

If you don't know how or think you can't, teach yourself how to do so and find a way in the midst of stressful forces in your environment. Find a way when there is tension building all around you.

This *relax* does not mean the type usually thought of when one flops down and relinquishes all physical activity in the "couch potato" mode. This *relax* means letting go of the tension you are feeling about or in any situation, getting off the electric path of the situation, turning "it" over to the Goddess to handle in the midst of your activity, although you continue in the physical demonstration of the activity. Allow the Goddess to speak through you although it is your lips that physically form the words.

HOW DOES IT FEEL?

Anxiety about what to do and say leaves you. Your words become completely coherent. Your consciousness is calm and receptive. If you are speaking and responding in a group of people, your "listening power" magnifies.

What you *thought* you heard now becomes crystal clear *knowing* what you heard. Into the other person's perspective, you gain complete insight. Nothing that is said frightens you. Your consciousness receives without simultaneously preparing a response.

When you verbally respond, you are crystal clear in your meaning. Although not in agreement with all that another says, hostility is absent from your response. Sounds crazy; even so, the more you do this the more you will feel at one with sensuality.

~ *My Own Understanding* ~

The rational mind would rather not contend with passion. Passion, unleashed, is an empowering force and can drive the rational mind to execute irrational acts.

2) Allure—
Be as one with your desire.

Step into the personae of your desire. Be it. Allure is the art of being it. Work with the law of the universe that likes attract likes. The more you can be the personae of your desire, the more you are into the energy of allure.

The law of magnetism is one that pulls itself to itself. The more often and the stronger your identification and merger with your desire, the sooner you will have it physically materialize.

HOW DOES IT FEEL?

Great. For the duration of the time you hold the desired personae in your consciousness, you feel exactly as having your desire will cause you to feel. Exactly.

~ *My Own Understanding* ~

Being in the role of your desire will give you a vignette of what you will get if you allow your desire to manifest on the physical plane.

3) Believe in the power of the receptive.

HOW DOES IT FEEL?

Believing in the power of the receptive gives you the feeling of quiet anticipation. It is the feeling that you have when you have been promised something by a person that experience has taught you always keeps their promises to you. You wait and are joyful while you wait because you know whatever has been promised is forthcoming.

Believing in the power of the receptive empowers you to handle other personal agenda items knowing to prepare for receiving your desire.

~ *My Own Understanding* ~

For an activist, the power of the receptive is an illusion with zero substance created for the mental comfort of the pacifist.

4) Resolve.

Be determined to stay on The Goddess path. This one is difficult only because in early development of magnetism you will want to come out of receive and go into acquire. This one is the blend of reason and passion. Keep the two in balance with each other. Do not allow passion to control reason. Do not allow reason to control passion. Remain in receptive mode.

HOW DOES IT FEEL?

At this stage, it feels conflicted. The deeper your habituation for assertion and acquiring through direct action, the stronger will be your urge to go into acquire mode. Rather like "riding out" any other addiction, ride out your addiction to the "go out and acquire" mode.

~ *My Own Understanding* ~

Blended well and in balance with each other, reason and passion's progeny are well suited to foil sabotage of self and others.

5) Intensify.

Active waiting intensifies your magnetism.

HOW DOES IT FEEL?

Active waiting is to wait while knowing that your desire is on its way because your magnetism is increasing. It is not the concept of passivity: "Oh well, I can't get what I want anyway, so I'll be quiet and maybe I will be blessed." No. Intensifying your magnetism feels like you are increasing the magnet component of your being. Turn up your "I am a magnet to . . ." thermostat and have the feeling of "It's on its way. Yeah, I have it." Enjoy the *invincibility* of magnetism and the power of the magnetic.

~ *My Own Understanding* ~

Intensification is like a brood hen. The longer she sits the warmer become the eggs. Enough heat spread over enough time (the season for hatching) inevitably yields the chicks for which she has been actively waiting.

6) Acknowledge the power of your sexual self.

Magnetize and pull with your butt and hips. Affirm the rhythm of your hips. Dance. Belly dancing, South American, African Tribal, and Hawaiian rhythms are especially good to develop the rhythm in your hips.

HOW DOES IT FEEL?

It feels like being beautiful and desirable in a sexual way without "working at it." It is not a feeling of efforting sexiness of behavior or looks. No efforting is involved. It is very simply a knowing that you are a sexual being and acknowledging that your sexuality feels powerful because it is powerful. It's the feeling that you get when you've done something funky and it was fun. It brought you joy and you'd do it again in spite of "conventional wisdom and tradition."

~ *My Own Understanding* ~

Once we claim and accept our sexual selves we empower ourselves to get beyond belief systems that label sex as something other than a gift from The One. As a friend of mine once said, "If God made anything better, he kept it to himself." I added . . . *and Mrs. God* and substituted *The One*. Then, the sentence reads: If The One made anything better, it was kept for God and Mrs. God.

7) Develop inner-self grace, elegance, poise and balance.

HOW DOES IT FEEL?

This one is very important. An earlier draft of this manuscript read: "This one is admittedly tough to describe other than to say that it's a feeling of no tension, no stress."

One of my friends who read this earlier draft was not satisfied. She didn't understand and insisted that I further elucidate. So back to Goddess I went. "Help me to describe further," I said.

Said She, "Description eludes because its a 'no feeling.' It's a feeling of, most importantly, *no panic.* In the outer world, the situation looks and feels awful, a foul-up that has the ability, *it seems,* to destroy some personal, already materialized, valued manifestation. Inner-self grace, elegance, poise, and balance take into account all outer world worst possibilities and simultaneously shield from inner panic as well as inner tension and stress."

Some people refer to a *fear-based reality*. I occasionally see what I refer to as a *reality-based fear,* i.e., *it's time to be afraid.* Accepting the bounty of your soul's inner-self grace, elegance, poise, and balance allows you to plan, then work your plan by acting in a way that changes external reality for you while at the same time shielding you from your own panic that would otherwise cause you to jump on your horse and ride off in all directions. (If you have never experienced almost panic from an outer reality about to overwhelm you, don't attempt the knowing. Enough Goddess path and you may never know. Be thankful. If you have experienced a panic attack or an almost one, you know the feeling. Never again. Reach for your bottle of Goddess inner-self grace, elegance, poise and balance.)

The physical materialization feeling is that of being out in the blazing hot sun, coming upon a garden-type fountain in the middle of the town square, and simply dipping your hand in. The feeling of coolness on your hand that for this moment soothes you throughout is the feeling of "no panic." Or, it is the feeling of having an extremely dry mouth and throat and popping a peppermint into your mouth and feeling the cooling as it dissolves into your throat. Neither is an air-conditioned building or a glass of water. Both allow you to pause, plan how to get to either and direct yourself to the building or the water.

8) Be prepared to receive the bountiful
good that flows into your life.

Open your heart to receive.

HOW DOES IT FEEL?

The feeling is one of quiet joy, like you feel when you know something
good is about to happen. You just don't know what.

~ *My Own Understanding* ~

Get ready to run through the candy store like a kid whose dentist approves.

9) Softly, gently, and tenderly refine the manifestation of your desire.

Smooth away any rough edges.

HOW DOES IT FEEL?

Notice that you are refining the manifestation of your desire. So, that which you magnetized has arrived. You have it! Refining on The Goddess path feels like being satisfied with your manifestation as it contemporaneously becomes more and more of what you desire and less and less separate and apart from you. You absorb your manifestation into your being and your manifestation absorbs your being. The absorption is the feeling of "no place like home" after a long trip. The comfort of feeling, touching and seeing familiar things and people.

~ *My Own Understanding* ~

Like with a kid's play dough, sculpt gently.

10) Watch and wait.

HOW DOES IT FEEL?

This guidance feels like you feel when you are thinking about many things and doing many things while you have a particular one in mind that you are not acting upon.

That "I'm getting there" feeling is the feeling of watching and waiting.

~ *My Own Understanding* ~

Let go, let Goddess.

11) Intensify the interconnectedness between your mental awareness and your heart's desire.

Gratify self-enhancing emotional needs.

HOW DOES IT FEEL?

Like knowing what you want and knowing it's appropriate to want it without having devoted intense thought to the desire and whether it is "good for you."

~ *My Own Understanding* ~

Trust the intensely rich fiber of your own soul to guide you.

12) Cherish your understanding.

Cherish your beloved.

HOW DOES IT FEEL?

Now that you have the bounty, it is the feeling of enjoying the joy and the happiness. It is the feeling of satisfaction that you get when you know an outfit has been perfectly accessorized. It is the elegance brought to the masculine by an elegant feminine that smoothes and colors the dimension.

~ *My Own Understanding* ~

Humans treasure too little. Cherishing energy is powerfully motivating.

13) Know. Succor. Pray. Integrate all.

HOW DOES IT FEEL?

It feels like practicing what you preach, walking your talk.

~ *My Own Understanding* ~

Through integration comes balance.

VALUE THE DOING OF YOUR DESIRE.

Know that you and only you arrange the energies in your universe to materialize as you desire. Whatever you truly desire materializes exactly as you would have it. Have it your way.

You do by desiring. Silence is centering and materializing from the doing of desire mode. Center inside your being, inside your essence, inside your spirit, inside your soul and desire freely and intensely.

To value the doing by desire is as crucial to The Goddess Way as is accepting the bounty of your soul.

~ My Own Understanding ~

Her doing is easy.

~ *How to value the doing of desire:* ~

14) Merriment

Gaiety is magnetic. Intensely so, for materializing from the doing of desire mode.

~ *My Own Understanding* ~

All the world loves a lover. Surely, gloom and doom in the *misery loves company* mode are not desirable. Magnetize your desires from the *merriment loves company* mode.

15) Elegance

Elegant expression of self. Svelte expression.

~ My Own Understanding ~

Uncluttered communication.

16) Calm

Stillness. To allow the doing of desire, calmness and stillness are crucial. Simply be still and desire.

~ My Own Understanding ~

Meditate on breath in and out.

17) Fixity of Purpose

Sureness that you will receive what you want. Be aware of the absolute safety and security in the doing of desire.

"You will decide on a matter and it will be established for you and the light shall shine upon thy ways."

(Job 23:28)

Stay on path. Stay with purpose.

~ My Own Understanding ~

Keep your eyes on the prize.

18) Observe and accumulate your realized desires that you obtained through desiring.

Build through quietness your personae of magnetism. Reach for nothing from your mate. Pull. Desire it and pull. Stay in receive mode and pull.

~ My Own Understanding ~

When you inventory your desires that you have pulled to you and manifested into physical form without conscious practice, you more clearly understand the power of the magnetic. It then is easier to stay in receive.

19) Goal accomplished.
Desire manifested.

Connect with your desire. See, know, feel when your desire has been realized. Make room for your desire before it materializes in the physical.

~ *My Own Understanding* ~

Give your intuition permission to inform you when your desire is on its way and will arrive soon.

HEALING

A Major Initiation on the Path. Grand. Majestic. A healing of psyche wounds. Claim your desire. Claim that which is yours. Claim your good as yours.

Allow yourself to claim and accept the joy of freedom from pain of any sort—mental, emotional, or physical.

~ *How to:* ~

20) Gratitude. Appreciation. Peace.

Be still. Look at every desire you've ever had and its manifested fulfillment. Appreciate how your desire has materialized.

Be joyful. Create no crisis. Sit quietly in the abundance of all that you have. No running away to create more crisis for excitement. Accept the benefit of having excitement from joy.

~ *My Own Understanding* ~

Cease habituation to the adrenaline rush that comes from the excitement of crisis.

21) Treasure your inner peace.

Be steadfast in refusing to allow negativity into your being and your environment. Avail yourself of all the benefits of systemic protection you have developed.

~ *My Own Understanding* ~

Cease applying salt to the wound.

22) Prestige

Enjoy it. To be working this path, you've earned it. Be as still as water in a lake when it's not moving.

~ *My Own Understanding* ~

Accept the esteem bestowed upon you by others. Using the power of receiving, you will have made it look so easy.

23) Exhibit inner tenacity.

Move out and keep out worry and trepidation from your soul and spirit.
(Synonyms for trepidation are apprehension, disquiet, alarm, and anxiety.)

~ *My Own Understanding* ~

After the 1996 Olympics, who will not remember, "Stick the landing"?
So, stick the landing!

24) Have a sensuous soul.

Your soul sings. Some will want to know how it is possible to have a sensuous soul. It is easy this far on the path of the Goddess. To travel the path of the Goddess, a sensuous soul cannot be avoided.

~ *My Own Understanding* ~

A sensuous soul is one aware of the nuances in living.

25) Appreciate the substance of magnetism.

The substance of magnetism is substantial. The essential feminine is the core of magnetism. Dance. Allow your soul and spirit to dance.

The dance of the magnetic is pure allure. It cannot be resisted.

~ *My Own Understanding* ~

The pulling of magnetism, rather than the achieving principle, evokes the soft, tender, and gentle feminine of the person with whom you are communicating. Likes magnetize likes. Softness, tenderness, and gentleness are substantial.

26) Heal yourself of stress reactions of the body more and more by saying a "whatever" to issues and situations that are not yours.

Detach. Decentralize. Relinquish control of everyone but yourself. The more you relinquish control, the more you give up fearing the unknown and thereby rub the balm of serenity on your psyche. Accept the refuge of your inner sanctum. Accept your own power as immeasurable.

~ My Own Understanding ~

Pick your battles.

27) Inventory your wherewithal.

Like any other enterprise, keep your outgo and your input balanced.

~ *My Own Understanding* ~

Evaluate your strong suits and your areas requiring helpful development.

28) Sanguineous

Sanguineous means *warmth*; an ardent spirit. I thought of changing this word like I thought of changing "bounty." Other words don't quite reach this energy. She said, "Sanguineous" and that is what She means. Let the energy of sanguineous be your calling card.

~ *My Own Understanding* ~

Warmth magnetizes. Hostility repels.

29) Pay no regard to disregard of your essence and your self.

Allow your soul the strength of confidence. Life with exhilaration in it is pleasurable.

~ My Own Understanding ~

Ignore harmful detractors of your soul yearnings.

30) Odyssey

The soul's journey on the planet is an odyssey of experiences. As we understand that experience is all that it is, an experience over which we have total dominion, then our lives truly become our tapestry to weave as we will.

~ My Own Understanding ~

Be in charge of your own life.

31) Validate your own feelings.

Listen to the whispers of your soul so that you don't have to listen to the shouts. If there is discontent in the soul, pay attention. You'll hear why.

~ My Own Understanding ~

No matter that you are programmed to believe that your feelings are not important, they are.

32) Trust the yearnings of your soul to guide you on this path.

Do what you need to do to satisfy soul yearnings. This action is always the right action. More good coming your way. Expect only the good to be in your life, an abundance of it.

Listen to the whispers of your soul. Trust the whispers. Pay attention. You will hear why.

Sit quietly. Adjust to the phenomenon of being desired and not having to reach out. Your task now will be to narrow your acceptance of who gets in. You may have prestige if you desire it.

~ *My Own Understanding* ~

Simply pull that which is soul satisfying.

BE DESIRABLE AND DESIRED.

Sit quietly. Adjust to the phenomenon of being desired and not having to reach out. Your task now will be to narrow your acceptance of who gets into your inner circle.

~ My Own Understanding ~

Be hard to get.

33) Titillate.

Be provocative in your quietness. Remember the value of silence and quietness. Have fun with this one. You'll get multiple offers.

~ My Own Understanding ~

Silence is a power rarely used as a power. Use it once you have expressed your desires.

34) Be a beacon.

Beacons of light are calm, steady and consistent. Be calm, steady and consistent in your knowingness of your desirability and your succor of those around you.

~ My Own Understanding ~

It's OK that others seek you out to bask in your light. Even so, keep negativity out of your inner circle of those around you.

35) Play.

Play along with experiences as they present themselves. Express your own soul's desire and thinking within each experience. Live each experience. Not rushing. Simply moving along with the experience.

~ *My Own Understanding* ~

Play validates and nurtures the kid in you.

36) Dynasty

Queenship. The dynasty of the diamond. Many faceted, brilliance, clarity. Cuts glass. A composite of the earth's mineral. Blended into pricelessness. Having a dynasty is being a queen in your soul. Accepting homage for your soul. A queen in your own right who is free of jealousy of other queens and their territories.

~ My Own Understanding ~

I am.

37) Joy and Rapture

Enter the universe of symbiosis. Joy and rapture do benefit each other. See straight ahead. See always the interconnection—the nexus. The nexus is always there because of the unity in the universe.

~ *My Own Understanding* ~

    Experiencing the nexus of two highly spiritual emotions is a triumph of the spirit.

38) What To Do?

Take a break. Breathe. As in exhale. Take a breather.

~ *My Own Understanding* ~

Rest and respite are invaluable.

39) Rest in the light.

Look for underneath meanings.

~ *My Own Understanding* ~

Resting in the light is a wonderful time to receive revelations.

40) Courage and Valor

Listen. Be agnostic. Question. Courage is very interesting here. What it requires is valor enough to stand on your position that has been assumed in the first place because of your soul urgings.

JOAN R. TARPLEY

~ *My Own Understanding* ~

Taking a stand and sticking the landing requires courage, not bravado.

41) Vintage

Accept yourself as vintage wine. Priceless and to be savored by only the appreciative.

~ *My Own Understanding* ~

Be special and accept being treated as special.

42) Proxy

Allow others who are sufficiently attuned to your way and your methodology to act for you. This is crucial to the doing by desire and the law of magnetism.

~ *My Own Understanding* ~

Delegate to those who understand and believe in your mission.

43) Have a good one.

A quiet restful day is one of the best therapeutics for the soul. As little as possible discourse and exchange with other people, especially do not engage in discourse that is not fun and loving.

~ *My Own Understanding* ~

Silence understood as no obligation for social discourse allows the conscious mind a respite.

44) Financial Momentum

Appreciate the value of financial wherewithal and support.

~ My Own Understanding ~

Express or feel no disdain for wealth for the sake of disdaining wealth.

45) Propagate.

Be a cheerleader for the way of the Goddess.

~ *My Own Understanding* ~

Quietly state the message of Goddess if asked.

46) Be percipient.

(A keen perspective.) Develop the keenness of your perspective. The keener your perspective, the more able you are to differentiate the perspectives of other persons.

~ My Own Understanding ~

Intuition helps.

47) Opportune

Jump in. See the advantage within situations to further the best interests of your soul.

~ *My Own Understanding* ~

Cease to await what you view as a perfect situation. Accept an opportunity for what it is and allow the nurturing of your soul.

48) Not to worry about anything.

You will not be alone.

~ *My Own Understanding* ~

Worry is neither electrically active nor magnetically receptive. So why do it?

49) Bank your resources.

Have a reservoir of power to draw on. Treat your inner resources as you would your money in the bank.

~ *My Own Understanding* ~

It is important to expend your resources with wisdom.

50) Make withdrawals wisely.

Invest in the people that invest positively in you. Other people who nurture, support, and cherish your energies are precious "others" on your spiritual path.

~ My Own Understanding ~

Why make withdrawals of your resources for the unappreciative? Contribute your resources to those who would do the same for you.

Rounding Out

Volume One is at an end. I went to plead OUR cause to the Goddess. "More please," I said. I had particular reference to the work on *Intimacy* with its section on "Romance and Mating" that She already had me writing before I went back to write "My Own Understandings" for Volume One.

"May I please include the writings on *Intimacy*?"

She answered me thusly, "The purpose of Volume One is to ground its readers solidly in the magnetic. Grounding is to the magnetic as grounding is to the electric. With a good grounding, the rest is easy. A good solid grounding allows for the complete receptivity so vital for intimacy and the creativity that follows in Volume Three. With segments, readers are not overwhelmed by trying to do it all at one time. Volumes One and Two and Three are sequential. If kept to volumes, each is affordable by everyone and none of the material is skipped or scanned without full understanding while in a rush to get to the next topic."

So be it. I suggest that you read this volume in its entirety as you would any other book. Then go back and meditate on and try on one guidance a week, moving sequentially one through fifty. That will require fifty weeks the first year you're working on the magnetic path and give you a two-week respite.

If you are anything like me, you won't do that. You will want to go faster. So, the next best progression is to meditate on and try on no more than a guidance per day. Go along at your own speed. When you come to a guidance that requires more than one day to understand—and you will—allow yourself the days you need to assimilate and understand. In this way, you are travelling at your own pace and gaining mastery.

A word on mastery. Mastery of the magnetic is the goal the Goddess has established for each of us. The ability to be equally magnetic and electric and be either one as appropriate for the life experience we are having makes us whole. Wholeness of self is vitally important for the next volume, *Intimacy*. The more whole you are while being intimate with another person who is whole at the level you are functioning, the better it is. Then comes the day that you are whole enough to be almost whole being intimate with a person who is almost whole. That's the day you will say: "It doesn't get any better than this."

And of course, one day it does, whether with the same person, with another person or in another situation. It is then you realize you are gaining mastery and you have moved to a "more better" dimension. Gaining mastery spirals you higher and higher and closer and closer to the Goddess herself until one day you actually touch and see her as well as feel her presence.

The only "better" I have discovered beyond touching and seeing the

Goddess whenever I desire the experience in my heart is that of seeing, touching, and feeling The One via her path.

Seeing, touching, and feeling The One with the receptivity the Goddess has taught you is to be blissed out.